Math Card Games

Grades 2–3

by

Claire Piddock

Published by Ideal School Supply
an imprint of
Frank Schaffer Publications®

TM

ideal
school supply

Author: Claire Piddock
Editor: Karen Thompson

Frank Schaffer Publications®

Ideal School Supply is an imprint of Frank Schaffer Publications.

Send all inquiries to:
Frank Schaffer Publications
3195 Wilson Drive NW
Grand Rapids, Michigan 49544

Math Card Games—grades 2–3

ISBN: 0-7424-3012-X

1 2 3 4 5 6 7 8 9 10 PAT 10 09 08 07 06 05

Table of Contents

Introduction to the Games

Students like to play games, and students like to win. Their parents and teachers like them to practice math facts, to stretch and organize their thinking, and to develop social skills. The math card games in this book can satisfy the needs of students, parents, and teachers. First, each game provides practice using mathematical concepts, such as adding, subtraction, multiplying, and dividing, identifying fractions and geometric shapes, or counting money. Second, each game encourages students to develop higher-level thought processes, such as making and testing hypotheses or organizing data. Third, most games are played in groups, giving students the opportunity to work together amicably and mediate differences when needed.

Drill and Practice

Use the math card games to review basic addition and subtraction and drill basic multiplication and division facts in ways that are interesting and challenging to students. While students may balk at memory-testing tasks such as flash cards, they will participate eagerly in activities that allow them to compete and win. You should remember that these games have not been designed to introduce or explain the mathematical concepts and skills for which they provide practice. However, relevant vocabulary and illustrations are provided in the teacher/parent section of each game, if applicable.

Higher-Level Thinking

Success in these card games involves some luck, some memory, and some strategy. Students realize that luck is involved, but as they experience the games, they begin to see ways to maximize the effects of good luck or minimize the effects of bad luck. They begin to think about what can happen, what is most likely to happen, and how they can take advantage of different outcomes. In short, they develop strategies. Then, they collect information about how successful their strategies were and, when necessary, revise those strategies.

Teaching the Games

Introduce the games to small groups of students. You may want to watch as they play to be sure that everyone understands the rules. At other times, you might play with them to model how to play the game. Once a few students understand a game, they can teach it to others. The teacher-parent page includes suggestions for teaching and variations of the game. Encourage students to extend the game, suggest variations, or create their own games.

0-7424-3012-X Math Card Games

Introduction continued

Preparing Materials

Each game includes a description of how to make the cards needed for that game. Students can help prepare the cards. You can purchase ready-made decks of blank cards or use plain or colored index cards. Cut-out pieces of poster board in card-size rectangles will work, too. Black or bright color nylon or felt-tip markers can be used for writing on the cards, but be careful that the colors do not seep through the cards.

Additional materials are needed for some games. *Rolling Out the Facts* on page 7 requires a pair of dice. You might use number cubes as a substitute. For *Order Up Good Times* on page 21, each player needs some sort of stand with slots for cards. You can create one with styrofoam or wood. You might also be able to create slots for cards using envelopes stapled to cardboard or tag board.

Various blank equation forms for *Equation Train* on page 36 can be drawn on paper and multiple copies made beforehand, as can the box grids for *Build a Number* on page 48. *Equation Points* on page 39 requires the use of an egg timer or some other easily set device. For the coin shapes needed for coin cards in *Money Target* on page 61, you may wish to purchase toy money to tape to the cards. You can also make multiple copies of the coins shown on page 64, cut them out, and tape them to blank cards. Finally, a yardstick is needed for *Inchworm* on page 58.

Storing Materials

Materials for each game can be kept in clearly labeled plastic zippered bags of various sizes. Freezer bags will allow you to label the outside with the name of the game. Designate an area of the classroom as the Math Game Center if you do not already have a math center. Some games can be played alone. You may want to make multiples of those games and allow individual students to keep them in their work stations.

0-7424-3012-X Math Card Games

Group 1:
Addition and Subtraction—
Basic Facts Review

Students develop an understanding of number operations gradually. At first, they count individual objects; then they associate sets of objects such as with numbers. They learn the symbols and words for the numbers. Later they compare and order numbers, and learn to operate on them in various ways.

By the time students use these card games, addition and subtraction will be familiar operations. You can expect them to know basic addition facts up to 9 + 9 and basic subtraction facts up to 18 – 9.

The multiplication and division facts for numbers 0 through 9 will be less familiar, but students will have had experience with counting groups of equal numbers of objects to develop an understanding of multiplication facts. For example:

2 groups of 5 = 10

2 x 5 = 10

They also may have separated groups to model division. For example:

15 objects divided into 3 equal groups = 5 in each group

15 ÷ 3 = 5

The first three games in this group provide practice and review of basic addition and subtraction facts. The fourth game is offered to practice all four basic operations. However, any of the games can be extended or adapted to practicing multiplication and division facts.

Students roll two dice in *Rolling Out the Facts*. Then, they read the number and use digit cards to make the sum that was rolled. They attempt to use up all their digit cards making addition facts. This game can be played individually as well as with a group.

In *On the Nose,* students turn over cards and must use the exposed numbers to reach a target number. They practice adding two, three, or more numbers to reach the target.

In *Using Number Pairs,* students use the two numbers on a card to find a sum and a difference. This game can be extended to multiplication and division.

In *Trading Facts,* students attempt to collect eight cards with operations that have the same answer.

  0-7424-3012-X Math Card Games

Rolling Out the Facts

Concept: Reviewing basic addition and subtraction facts

Players: 1 or more

Materials: Prepare one set of ten digit cards for each player. The cards have the digits 0, 1, 2, 3, 4, 5, 6, 7, 8 and 9, one per card as follows:

A pair of dice.

Vocabulary:

The single numbers 0 through 9 are called *digits*.

The *sum* is the answer in an addition example.

8 + 7 = 15 <— sum

The *difference* is the answer in a subtraction example.

12 – 7 = 5 <— difference

Suggestions:

• This game can be played individually by one student or played by two or more students as a competition.

• To play the game individually, a player begins again with the ten cards, rolls the dice again, and repeats their "turn" in an attempt to use up all of their digit cards to make sums and differences. A player wins the game by using all of their cards.

• You might have a "silent" competition in which any student with free time can play the game individually and record their scores on a master sheet. At the end of the week, compute the total of the lowest five scores of each player who played at least five games. The person with the lowest total wins.

Variation 1: Roll three dice to find the target sum or difference.

Variation 2: Use the digit cards to make multiplication as well as addition and subtraction facts.

Rolling Out the Facts

Play with 1 or more players.

Each player rolls the dice to see who goes first. The player with the highest sum goes first. In case of a tie, the tied players roll again.

How to Deal:

• The first player lays out the ten digit cards face up.

• The first player rolls the dice.

Goal of the Game:

Use as many digit cards as possible to make sums and differences. The leftover cards add up to your score in each round. Have the lowest total at the end of the game.

To Begin Play:

• The first player adds the top numbers on the rolled dice. That is the target number.

• The player uses two digit cards in an addition or subtraction fact to make the target number.

Example: Suppose you roll a 2 and a 4. The sum is 6. Look for cards that make a sum or difference of 6.

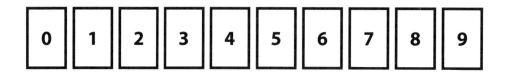

| 0 | 1 | 2 | 3 | 4 | 5 | 6 | 7 | 8 | 9 |

0-7424-3012-X Math Card Games

Rolling Out the Facts

Continue Play:

- Turn over two cards at a time that make the target sum or difference.

Example continued: If you rolled a sum of 6,

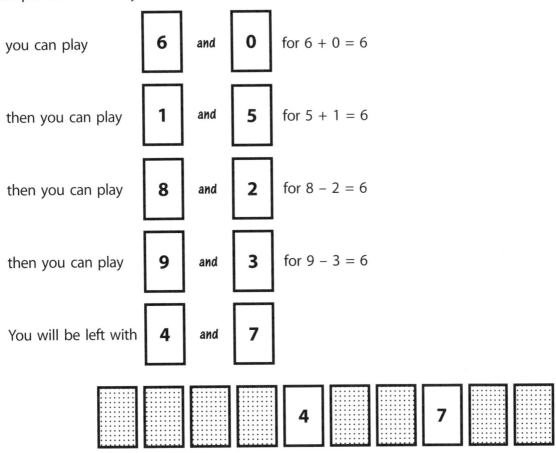

you can play **6** *and* **0**   for 6 + 0 = 6

then you can play **1** *and* **5**   for 5 + 1 = 6

then you can play **8** *and* **2**   for 8 − 2 = 6

then you can play **9** *and* **3**   for 9 − 3 = 6

You will be left with **4** *and* **7**

- Roll the dice again and turn over more cards, if you can use them to make the new target number.

- When you cannot use your face-up cards any more, your turn is over. Add the remaining face-up cards. That number is your score.

Example continued: Suppose you roll again and get top numbers of 6 and Your target number is 10. You cannot make 10 with your remaining cards of 4 and 7. Your turn is over. Your score for this round is 4 + 7 or 11.

- Play moves to the next person to the left. The player rolls the dice and begins with the ten face-up digit cards again.

Winning:

After all players have had a turn (or an equal number of turns), the winner is the player with the *lowest* total score.

0-7424-3012-X Math Card Games

On the Nose

Concept: Reviewing basic addition facts

Players: 2 or 3

Materials: Prepare four sets of ten digit cards.

| 0 | 1 | 2 | 3 | 4 | 5 | 6 | 7 | 8 | 9 |

Suggestions:

- *Variation 1:* This game uses addition facts to make a target number of 21. You may want to include basic subtraction facts, also. The rules are the same except that cards can be added to make a sum greater than 21. However, whenever a sum greater than 21 occurs, the next player must subtract numbers to get to the target 21.

- *Variation 2:* You may wish to extend the game to greater numbers. For example, have players aim for the number 35 instead of 21.

- *Variation 3:* You can have students use basic multiplication or multiplication and division facts as well as addition and subtraction facts to arrive at the goal number.

On the Nose

Play with 2 or 3 players.

Choose one person as dealer.

Dealer shuffles the cards.

How to Deal:

- Give three cards, face down, to each player.

- Place the deck in the center of the table face down.

- Players hold the cards in their hands so only they can see them.

To Begin Play:

- The player to the left of the dealer plays one of their cards face up in the middle of the table and takes the top card off the deck.

Goal of the Game:

The player who puts the last card down to make a sum of 21 wins the game.

first card

0-7424-3012-X Math Card Games

On the Nose

Continue Play:

- Play moves to the left around the table.

second card

- If you are the next player, choose one of the cards in your hand and place it on top of the face-up card in the middle of the table. Then, announce the sum of the two face-up cards.

- The third player adds another card from his or her hand the two face-up cards and adds its number to the previous sum. Then, they take the top card from the deck.

- Play continues in the same way around the table. On your turn, you look for a number that, when added to the previous sum, will make a total of 21. If you can make 21, you win the game!

- If you cannot make a sum of 21, add a card that makes the total less than 21. You cannot play a number that makes the sum greater than 21. You put down a card and take the top card from the deck.

- If you do not have a card that you can play, you pass, but you still must take the top card from the deck.

- If a player announces the wrong sum, the player must take back his card and lose a turn.

Winning:

third card

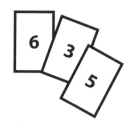

The winner is the person to put down the last number that will make the sum 21.

Using Number Pairs

Concept: Reviewing basic addition and subtraction facts

Players: 2 to 4

Materials: Prepare 45 cards in the pattern shown here.

Vocabulary:

The answer to an addition is called the *sum*.

8 + 7 = 15 <— sum

The answer to a subtraction is called the *difference*.

15 - 7 = 8 <— difference

Suggestions:

- Before students play the game, explain that students should think of two facts for each card—an addition fact and a subtraction fact. For example, the card with 9 on top and 3 on the bottom has two numbers associated with it:

    12 because 9 + 3 = 12 and

    6 because 9 – 3 = 6

- Emphasize with students that the numbers must be used in the order that they appear—the top number first and the bottom number second.

- *Variation:* You can extend this game to have students practice multiplication and division facts. In that case, some cards will have only three values associated with them. Division problems with remainders are not used.

1 1

2 1	2 2

3 1	3 2	3 3

4 1	4 2	4 3	4 4

5 1	5 2	5 3	5 4	5 5

6 1	6 2	6 3	6 4	6 5	6 6

7 1	7 2	7 3	7 4	7 5	7 6	7 7

8 1	8 2	8 3	8 4	8 5	8 6	8 7	8 8

9 1	9 2	9 3	9 4	9 5	9 6	9 7	9 8	9 9

Using Number Pairs

Play with 2, 3, or 4 players.

Choose one person as dealer.

Dealer shuffles the cards.

How to Deal:

• Give five cards to each player.

• Put the rest of the deck in the center of the table. Turn the top card face up and place it next to the deck.

Each card has a top number and a bottom number. Use the top and bottom numbers in order to find a sum or a difference. These are the "values."

Example: if the first face-up card is $\boxed{\begin{array}{c} \mathbf{8} \\ \mathbf{2} \end{array}}$ it has the values 10 and 6.

    10 because 8 + 2 = 10

     6 because 8 − 2 = 6

Players hold their cards so no one else can see them.

Goal of the Game:

Be the first player to use up all of your cards.

To Begin Play:

• The player to the left of the dealer goes first.

• The player looks for any card in their hand that has one of the same values as the face-up card in the middle.

0-7424-3012-X Math Card Games

Using Number Pairs

- You play any card that has a value of the face-up card. If
  is the face-up card, look for a value of 10 or 6.

<table>
<tr><td>8</td></tr>
<tr><td>2</td></tr>
</table>

For example, if these are your cards, you can play

<table>
<tr><td>7</td></tr>
<tr><td>3</td></tr>
</table>

or

<table>
<tr><td>7</td></tr>
<tr><td>1</td></tr>
</table>

.

If you cannot play any card in your hand, draw cards from the center deck until you can play one. Play moves to the next person to the left.

Whenever a card is played, it becomes the new face-up card. The next player must match one of the values on the new face-up card.

If the deck is used up before there is a winner, the face-up cards—except for the top card—are reshuffled and used again.

Winning:

The winner is the first player to run out of cards.

<table>
<tr><td>7</td></tr>
<tr><td>3</td></tr>
</table>

because 7 + 3 = 10

<table>
<tr><td>3</td></tr>
<tr><td>2</td></tr>
</table>

<table>
<tr><td>4</td></tr>
<tr><td>4</td></tr>
</table>

<table>
<tr><td>9</td></tr>
<tr><td>5</td></tr>
</table>

<table>
<tr><td>7</td></tr>
<tr><td>1</td></tr>
</table>

because 7 − 1 = 6

0-7424-3012-X Math Card Games

Trading Facts

Concepts: Reviewing basic facts—all operations

Players: 4 to 6

Materials: Prepare one set of eight basic-fact example cards for each player. Make four sets if there are four players. Make six sets if there are six players.

All of the examples in a single set have the same answer.

Sample set for the number 7:

3 + 4	2 + 5	9 − 2	35 ÷ 5
16 − 9	6 + 1	63 ÷ 9	7 x 1

Sample set for the number 9:

3 x 3	3 + 6	7 + 2	18 − 9
16 − 7	54 ÷ 6	10 − 1	36 ÷ 4

You can make other sets of eight cards for the numbers 1, 2, 3, 4, 5, 6, 8, and 10.

Suggestions:

- Before beginning the game with students, you may want to challenge them to think of examples that have the same answer. Ask, "What examples will give you a sum, difference, product, or quotient of 7?" Answers can be the ones on the cards shown above or others such as 7 + 0, 14 ÷ 2, or 10 − 3.

- If students need extra practice in some of the operations, such as multiplication and division, you can limit the sets to these operations only.

Trading Facts

Play with 4, 5, or 6 players.

Choose one person as dealer.

Dealer shuffles the cards.

How to Deal:

• Give a card face down to each player until you use up the deck.

• Each player should have eight cards.

Players sort their cards, so cards having example with the same answers are together.

Example of how a player with these cards would sort them.

| These cards go together because their answer is 7. | These cards both have an answer of 10. | These have no match. |

Goal of the Game:

Be the first player to collect eight cards that have the same answer.

To Begin Play:

• Each player selects a number of cards that he or she is willing to trade. The cards are held face down and the number of cards available is called out. For example, if you have the cards above, you might want to trade the four cards on the right to try to collect the other cards that have an answer of 7.

0-7424-3012-X Math Card Games

Trading Facts

Continue Play:

- If you have four cards you want to trade, you call out "four" until you find someone to trade four cards with you.

- If no one wants to trade four cards, you can change to three, two, or one card until you find someone willing to trade.

- When a trade is completed, the players look at their new cards and sort them. Sort your cards again, decide which cards you want to keep, and then try for a new trade.

- Players continue until a player collects all eight of the cards that have the same answer.

Example: A winning set of cards might look like this:

3 + 4	2 + 5	9 – 2	35 ÷ 5
16 – 9	6 + 1	63 ÷ 9	7 x 1

- Here are some things to remember:

  ✓ Remember, you do not show the cards you are going to trade.

  ✓ You can change your mind before the trade is made.

  ✓ No one is forced to trade if they do not want to.

Winning:

The winner is the first player to collect a set of eight cards having the same answer.

0-7424-3012-X Math Card Games

Group 2:
Multiplication and Division Practice

Students are introduced to multiplication in terms of number of sets having an equal number of objects, and division as the reverse—dividing a group into a number of equal sets. Both operations can be modeled using an array.

You can use an array like the following as a model for multiplication and division:

4 rows of 6 = 24 dots in all	$4 \times 6 = 24$
6 columns of 4 = 24 dots in all	$6 \times 4 = 24$
24 separated into 4 equal rows = 6 in each row	$24 \div 4 = 6$
24 separated into 6 equal columns = 4 in each column	$24 \div 6 = 4$

Although the models are used to develop the concept, students will eventually commit the multiplication and division facts to memory. The following games will help students practice and recall basic multiplication and division facts. If they have difficulty, remind students of the models, either in pictures or concrete materials, that they can use to help them remember. Give students the following hints:

Hint 1: If they forget a multiplication fact, encourage students to use the order property. For example, if they forget 5×7, they might remember $7 \times 5 = 35$.

Hint 2: Encourage students to use doubles. If they know $2 \times 8 = 16$, they can double it to find $4 \times 8 = 32$.

Before beginning this set of games, remind students that any number times 1 is the number, and any number times 0 is 0. They should also know that 0 divided by any number is 0.

0-7424-3012-X Math Card Games

Group 2:
Multiplication and Division Practice
continued

The card games in this section focus on multiplication, division, or the combined operations.

Students find products and then place them in the correct order in *Order Up Good Times*. This game fosters strategic thinking in that the cards players receive are random, but students need to think about which products are yet to come so they can place their card in the appropriate place.

Division Trail is similar to a traditional dominoes game that students are likely to know. They look for matches to division examples or quotients. The cards have division example on the top and quotients on the bottom. Some cards have the correct example and quotient on the same card. These are called doubles. Most of the cards are not doubles. Students lay out the cards in dominoes fashion, so make sure they have enough space on their playing surface.

The game *Oops!* is played much like the traditional game *Old Maid*. The game is played where players avoid having the last unmatched card. You can prepare cards with multiplication facts, division facts, or both.

In *Slappy Number Pairs,* students must be quick thinkers and be the first to recognize a given product or quotient. Only two students can play at one time. It is best if they sit across from each other, but both must be able to reach the cards in the center of the table.

0-7424-3012-X Math Card Games

Order Up Good Times

Concepts: Using basic multiplication facts
Ordering numbers to 99

Players: 4

Materials: Prepare sets of eleven cards of
multiplication facts using factors of 0
through 10.

Examples:

A set of cards for facts 3: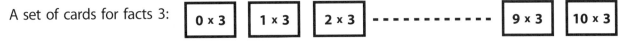

A set of cards for facts 4: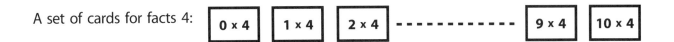

A set of cards for facts 5: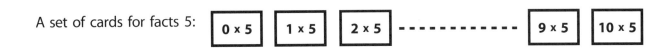

Select three sets for each game depending
on the multiplication facts students need to
practice.

Make three stands that will hold eight cards,
one in each slot. You can make them from
wood or styrofoam. You might also simply
staple 8 small envelopes vertically on a long
piece of oak tag or cardboard.

Suggestions:

• Review with students how to order numbers
to 99. Remind them to look at the tens place
first and compare. If the tens place is the
same, compare the digits in the ones place.

Examples:

45 is greater than 25 because
4 tens is greater than 2 tens

36 is greater than 33 because
6 ones is greater than 3 ones

• Be sure to let students know in advance
which three facts they will be practicing. You
can have them use the sets for facts of 3, 4,
and 5 or another three sets, such as the facts
for 7, 8, and 9.

Order Up Good Times

Play with 4 players.

Choose one person as dealer.

Dealer shuffles the cards.

How to Deal:

• Do not deal the cards after shuffling. Put the deck face down in the center of the table.

• A card stand is in front of each player, so that when cards are in the slots, you should be able to see only your own cards and no one else's cards.

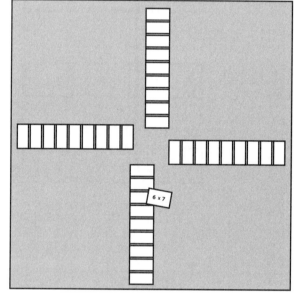

Goal of the Game:

Build a sequence of cards, so the products are in order. The product on each card must be greater than the one in front of it.

To Begin Play:

• The player to the left of the dealer goes first.

• Take the top card from the deck and place it in one of the slots.

Hint: Once a card is in a slot, you are not allowed to move it to another slot, so think ahead. Think about where the other products might go.

Order Up Good Times

Continue Play:

- Each player, in turn, draws a card from the deck and puts it in a slot.

- If you cannot play the card, you discard it face-up next to deck.

- Once there are cards in the discard pile, you can take the top card or draw from the deck.

- Although you cannot move cards from slot to slot, you can discard a card in a slot on your turn and draw a new card.

Here is what a correct order of eight cards might look like:

Winning:

The winner is the first player to fill all the slots in correct order.

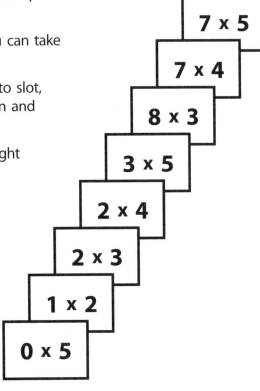

Division Trail

Concepts: Using basic division facts

Players: 2 or more

Materials: Prepare one each of these cards:

0 ÷ 1	0 ÷ 2	0 ÷ 3	0 ÷ 4	0 ÷ 5	0 ÷ 6	0 ÷ 7	0 ÷ 8	0 ÷ 9
0	1	2	3	4	5	6	7	8
1 ÷ 1	2 ÷ 2	3 ÷ 3	4 ÷ 4	5 ÷ 5	6 ÷ 6	7 ÷ 7	8 ÷ 8	9 ÷ 9
9	0	1	2	3	4	5	6	7
2 ÷ 1	4 ÷ 2	6 ÷ 3	8 ÷ 4	10 ÷ 5	12 ÷ 6	14 ÷ 7	16 ÷ 8	18 ÷ 9
8	9	0	1	2	3	4	5	6
3 ÷ 1	6 ÷ 2	9 ÷ 3	12 ÷ 4	15 ÷ 5	18 ÷ 6	21 ÷ 7	24 ÷ 8	27 ÷ 9
7	8	9	0	1	2	3	4	5
4 ÷ 1	8 ÷ 2	12 ÷ 3	16 ÷ 4	20 ÷ 5	24 ÷ 6	28 ÷ 7	32 ÷ 8	36 ÷ 9
6	7	8	9	0	1	2	3	4
5 ÷ 1	10 ÷ 2	15 ÷ 3	20 ÷ 4	25 ÷ 5	30 ÷ 6	35 ÷ 7	40 ÷ 8	45 ÷ 9
5	6	7	8	9	0	1	2	3
6 ÷ 1	12 ÷ 2	18 ÷ 3	24 ÷ 4	30 ÷ 5	36 ÷ 6	42 ÷ 7	48 ÷ 8	54 ÷ 9
4	5	6	7	8	9	0	1	2
7 ÷ 1	14 ÷ 2	21 ÷ 3	28 ÷ 4	35 ÷ 5	42 ÷ 6	49 ÷ 7	56 ÷ 8	63 ÷ 9
3	4	5	6	7	8	9	0	1
8 ÷ 1	16 ÷ 2	24 ÷ 3	32 ÷ 4	40 ÷ 5	48 ÷ 6	56 ÷ 7	64 ÷ 8	72 ÷ 9
2	3	4	5	6	7	8	9	0
9 ÷ 1	18 ÷ 2	27 ÷ 3	36 ÷ 4	45 ÷ 5	54 ÷ 6	63 ÷ 7	72 ÷ 8	81 ÷ 9
1	2	3	4	5	6	7	8	9

Suggestions:

- This is a dominoes-like game, so students should play on a table large enough to spread cards out side by side.

- Make sure students know that a double is a card that shows a division example and its answer.

0-7424-3012-X Math Card Games

Division Trail

Play with 2, 3, or 4 players.

Choose one person as dealer.

Dealer shuffles the cards.

How to Deal:

- Give three cards to each player. Place the deck face down in the middle of the table

- Players place the cards face up on the table in front of them.

The first deal might look like this:

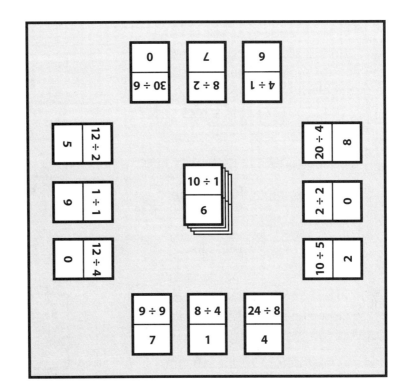

Goal of the Game:

Be the first player to put down all your cards.

To Begin Play:

- Play moves to the left.

- The first to have a *double* places it in the center of the table. If a player does not have a double, he or she must draw the top card until a double is found. A *double* is a division fact and its quotient on the same card.

These are the doubles to look for:

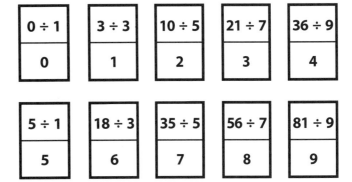

Division Trail

Continue Play:

- After the first double is played, you must match either the division example with a correct quotient, or the quotient with an example that has it as an answer. You can play either end.

Example:

Play any card with a 2 here.

Play any card with an example that has the quotient 2 here.

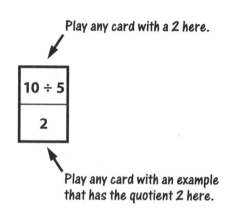

Play any card with a 2 here.

10 ÷ 5
2

Play any card with an example that has the quotient 2 here.

- If you cannot match the example or the difference, you must draw a card and place it face up in front of you with your other cards.

- Play moves to the next person to the left. You can play either end.

- If a player has a double that matches any end card, you place it horizontally, so the next players can match either end.

Example:

Player matched 2 with the division example 10 ÷ 5 because 10 ÷ 5 = 2.

Player matched the division 18 ÷ 9 with the number 2 because 18 ÷ 9 = 2.

Player matched the number 6 with a double, and plays the card crosswise.

Next player can play on either end.

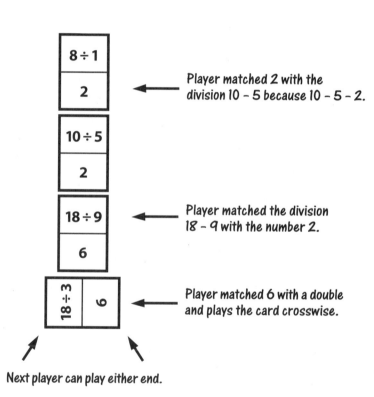

Player matched 2 with the division 10 – 5 because 10 – 5 – 2.

Player matched the division 18 – 9 with the number 2.

Player matched 6 with a double and plays the card crosswise.

Next player can play either end.

Winning:

The winner is the first player to play all of their cards.

Oops!

Concept: Using basic multi-plication/division facts

Players: 2 to 6

Materials: Prepare a set of paired cards for all the facts you wish to have students practice and one single card with "Oops!" on it.

Sample multiplication pairs

| 8 × 7 | 56 |

| 3 × 5 | 15 |

Sample division pairs

| 9 ÷ 9 | 1 |

| 21 ÷ 3 | 7 |

OOPS!

For example, if you wish to have students practice multiplication and division facts for 8, prepare cards for:

0 x 8, 8 x 0, and two cards showing the number 0

1 x 8, 8 x 1, and two cards showing the number 8

2 x 8, 8 x 2, and two cards showing the number 16

3 x 8, 8 x 3, and two cards showing the number 24

4 x 8, 8 x 4, and two cards showing the number 32

5 x 8, 8 x 5, and two cards showing the number 40

6 x 8, 8 x 6, and two cards showing the number 48

7 x 8, 8 x 7, and two cards showing the number 56

9 x 8, 8 x 9, and two cards showing the number 72

And:

72 ÷ 8 and a card for 9

64 ÷ 8 and a card for 8

56 ÷ 8 and a card for 7

48 ÷ 8 and a card for 6

40 ÷ 8 and a card for 5

32 ÷ 8 and a card for 4

24 ÷ 8 and a card for 3

16 ÷ 8 and a card for 2

8 ÷ 8 and a card for 1

Vocabulary:

The *product* is the answer in a multiplication example.

   4 x 5 = 20 <— product

The *quotient* is the answer to a division example.

   18 ÷ 6 = 3 <— quotient

Suggestions:

• *Variation:* You can vary the game to include as many (or as few) multiplication and/or division facts as desired.

0-7424-3012-X Math Card Games

Oops!

Play with 2, 3, 4, 5, or 6 players.

Choose one person as dealer.

Dealer shuffles the cards.

How to Deal:

• Give one card to each player around the circle face down until there are no cards left.

• It does not matter if players begin with an unequal number of cards.

Goal of the Game:

Avoid being the last player who ends up holding the Oops! card.

To Begin Play:

• Players pick up their cards and look for pairs of cards that match.

A match can be a multiplication example and its product.

Here are two examples:

| 2 x 7 | 14 |

| 1 x 5 | 5 |

A match can also be a division example and its quotient.

| 9 ÷ 9 | 1 |

• Each player puts down pairs of matching cards until they have only unmatched cards.

• Place the matched cards face up in front of you, so others can check for errors. Each player puts down pairs of matching cards until they have only unmatched cards.

Oops!

Continue Play:

- After all the players have put down their matches, the dealer takes one card from the hand of the player to the right, without looking.

- If the new card can be matched with a card left in the dealer's hand, the dealer puts down that match face up.

- The play moves to the player to the right.

- The player to the dealer's right takes a card from the hand of the player to their right and, if possible, pairs it with a card from his or her own hand.

- Play continues around the circle to the right, with each person taking a card and making a match, if possible.

- When a player loses all of their cards, they are a winner and drop out of the game.

- After a while, all of the cards will be matched except the Oops! card.

Winning:

This game has many winners and one loser—the player who ends up with the unmatched Oops! card.

Slappy Number Pairs

Concepts: Using basic facts

Players: 2

Materials: Prepare forty-five cards in the pattern shown:

1/1								
2/1	2/2							
3/1	3/2	3/3						
4/1	4/2	4/3	4/4					
5/1	5/2	5/3	5/4	5/5				
6/1	6/2	6/3	6/4	6/5	6/6			
7/1	7/2	7/3	7/4	7/5	7/6	7/7		
8/1	8/2	8/3	8/4	8/5	8/6	8/7	8/8	
9/1	9/2	9/3	9/4	9/5	9/6	9/7	9/8	9/9

0-7424-3012-X Math Card Games

Slappy Number Pairs

Suggestions:

• Before students play the game, explain that each card has several numbers associated with it—all possible answers to an addition, subtraction, multiplication, or division carried out with the numbers in the order that they appear.

For example, the card has four numbers associated with it:

    12 because 9 + 3 = 12

     6 because 9 − 3 = 6

    27 because 9 x 3 = 27

     3 because 9 ÷ 3 = 3

> **9**
> **3**

• Emphasize with students that the numbers must be used in the order that they appear—the top number first and the bottom number second. The result is that, in some cases, only three numbers are associated with the card.

For example, the card has three numbers:

    4 because 2 + 2 = 4 and 2 x 2 = 4

    0 because 2 − 2 = 0

    1 because 2 ÷ 2 = 1

> **2**
> **2**

• If the quotient of the numbers is not a whole number, it is not used.

For example, the card has three numbers associated with it.

    12 because 7 + 5 = 12

     2 because 7 − 5 = 2

    35 because 7 x 5 = 35

> **7**
> **5**

    There is no whole number quotient for 7 ÷ 5.

• Students must decide on a target number for each round. You may want to have them roll two dice or select a random card from cards numbered 1 to 12 to choose the target number.

• You may need to set a time limit of 5 or 10 minutes for this game.

Slappy Number Pairs

Play this game with a partner.

Choose a target number from 1 to 12. Partners must agree on the target number.

Choose one person as dealer.

Dealer shuffles the cards.

How to Deal:

- Give each player one card face-down until you run out of cards.

- Each player stacks their cards neatly in a pile.

Goal of the Game:

Be the player with the all the cards or the most cards when time is called.

To Begin Play:

- At the same time, both players turn over the top card from their deck. They must place the cards in the center of the table between them side by side.

Slappy Number Pairs

Continue Play:

- If the value of one of the cards in the center of the table is the target number, players try to be the first to cover that card with their hand.

- Remember to add, subtract, multiply, and divide the numbers, if possible, to find the card values.

For example, if 10 is the target number, these are some cards that can be slapped.

| 7 |
| 3 | because 7 + 3 = 10

| 5 |
| 2 | because 5 x 2 = 10

| 8 |
| 2 | because 8 + 2 = 10

If the target number is 4, here are some of the cards that can be slapped:

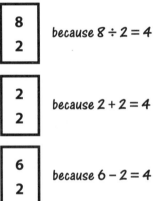

| 8 |
| 2 | because 8 ÷ 2 = 4

| 2 |
| 2 | because 2 + 2 = 4

| 6 |
| 2 | because 6 − 2 = 4

- The first player to cover the correct card collects both face-up cards and places them at the bottom of their stack.

- If neither player's card has the target number as its sum or difference, leave the cards there.

- Players turn up the next card in their stack, again at the same time. The first player to cover the target number wins all of the face-up cards.

Winning:

The winner is the player with all the cards or the most cards when time is called.

Group 3:
Numbers (including Fractions) and Algebra

The games in this section provide practice with fraction and algebra concepts. Using concrete models or pictures, students see fractions as part of a whole or part of a set. For example, $\frac{1}{3}$ can be pictured as one shaded area of a circle divided into three equal parts,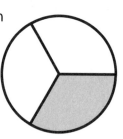

 or as one shaded square out of a set of three squares.

Students also use models to show that certain fractions are equivalent, that is, they name the same part.

These fraction strips show that $\frac{1}{2} = \frac{2}{4} = \frac{4}{8}$.

To reinforce these concepts, picture models and numbers are matched in these games.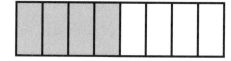

Algebra at this young age involves understanding properties of numbers and symbolic notations. In these games, students select numbers and/or operations to reach target values or to create equations. Blank equation forms to be filled, such as

give students experience with the concept of variables.

0-7424-3012-X Math Card Games

Group 3:
Numbers (including Fractions) and Algebra continued

The card games in this section provide practice using all operations with whole numbers, with operations symbols, and with identification of fractions and fraction equivalents.

In *Equation Train,* students begin with an addition equation in which the empty boxes are placeholders for numbers. They use the numbers that appear randomly on cards to fill the places, compute, and attempt to reach a target number. The equations can be varied to practice any operation or a combination of them.

Students also create equations in *Equation Points.* In this game, however, all players get the same ten numbers—the digits 0 through 9—and arrange them to make as many equations as possible. They receive points for the type of operations they use and a bonus for using all the numbers. Since using multiplication and division operations are worth more points than addition and subtraction problems, the game encourages practice with these two less familiar operations. This open-ended approach fosters creativity in problem solving and challenges students to make and test predictions about number combinations.

Fraction Match is a concentration-type game in which students match symbols for common fractions with pictures that model the fractions. Since the cards must be spread out, be sure students have a table with enough space for this game.

Fraction Fishin' focuses on matching equivalent fractions. In this game, students need to find matches for all the cards in their hands. You can use symbols only, or adapt the game to include fraction symbols accompanied by pictures, depending on the skill level of the players.

Build a Number challenges students to build the greatest three-digit number using the digits that appear randomly on the cards they draw. You can adapt the game to have players build the least three-digit number or build the greatest or least four-digit number.

0-7424-3012-X Math Card Games

Equation Train

Concepts: Creating and evaluating mathematical expressions
Comparing numbers to 99

Players: 2 or more

Materials: Prepare four each of the following digit cards:

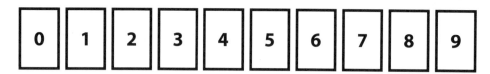

Prepare enough of the following expression
forms for each player:

□ + □   +   □ + □ ⟶ **20**

Suggestions:

- Before students begin, remind them to perform
the operations inside the parentheses first.

  For example: (3 + 4) + (6 + 2)

     7 + 8 = 15

- In this game, students fill the squares with
digit cards to make the target number. You
can create many variations of this game by
changing the target number and/or changing
the operations in the expressions.

  For example:

  □ + □   +   □ − □ ⟶ **6**

- Note that, when subtraction is involved, players will be disqualified from the game if they
create a subtraction that cannot be performed
such as:

  3 + 4   +   6 − 8 ⟶ **6**

- Here are some other equation
train forms that you may use:

  (□ − □) + (□ + □) ⟶ **10**

  (□ − □) + (□ × □) ⟶ **30**

  (□ × □) − (□ + □) ⟶ **15**

  (□ × □) − (□ − □) ⟶ **20**

  (□ + □) × (□ − □) ⟶ **30**

0-7424-3012-X Math Card Games

Equation Train

Play with 2 or more players.

Choose one person as dealer.

Dealer shuffles the digit cards.

How to Deal:

• Place the deck face-up in the middle of the table.

Goal of the Game:

Be the player to place digit cards so the sum is closest to the target number.

To Begin Play:

• The player to the left of the dealer copies the digit on the face-up card into any of his or her squares.

• Turn over the card and place it next to the deck.

□ + □   +   4 + 4 ⟶ 20

Example: The top card was a 4. Player wrote the 4 in a square and will turn over the digit card. The next player must use the digit 9.

Equation Train

Continue Play:

• The play continues around the circle to the left.

• Each player uses the digit on the face-up card by writing it in a square in front of them.

• You must think ahead to try to get a number equal to or close to the target number. Play continues until each player fills all the squares.

• Here is an example of results after 4 players finish.

Player 1 made the sum of 16. $3 + 4$ (16) $+$ $6 + 3$ ⟶ 20

Player 2 made the sum of 17. $2 + 0$ (17) $+$ $8 + 7$ ⟶ 20

Player 3 made the sum of 26. $9 + 4$ (26) $+$ $5 + 8$ ⟶ 20   *Player 3 wins this game!*

Player 4 made the sum of 28. $5 + 5$ (28) $+$ $6 + 2$ ⟶ 20

Winning:

The player whose equation gives an answer closest to or over the target number wins the game.

Equation Points

Concept: Writing equations

Players: 2 or 3 players

Materials: Prepare six sets of eleven cards. Each set has the numbers 0, 1, 2, 3, 4, 5, 6, 7, 8, 9, and 10, one per card.

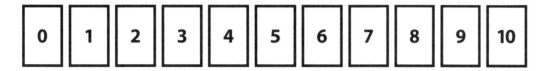

Make thirty each of the operations cards +, −, x, and ÷ and thirty cards with the = symbol.

Have a 3-minute egg timer available for each group of students playing the game.

Each student should have paper and pencil for writing equations. The dealer has the egg timer and a paper for scoring.

Make a chart or write on the board these point values:

Points Chart
Use all numbers = Bonus! 10 points
Use x = 5 points each
Use ÷ = 5 points each
Use + = 2 points each
Use − = 2 points each

Suggestions:

- Explain to students that, on their turn, they should use as many cards as possible to make equations. Display the points chart and explain the point values. They get 10 points for using all the cards in one or several equations. They get 5 points for every multiplication or division symbol used and 2 points for every addition or subtraction symbols used.

- Students should sit at a table with enough room for spreading out ten cards at a time and adding symbol cards between them.

- Tell students that they can add, subtract, multiply, or divide the numbers, but they cannot put two numbers together to make a 2-digit number. For example, they cannot use a 3 card and a 6 card to make 36 or 63.

Equation Points

Play with 3 players.

Choose one person as dealer.

In this game, the dealer gives out the cards and scores the game. The dealer does not make equations.

Dealer shuffles the number cards.

How to Deal:

- Give ten cards face down to each player. Put the deck aside.

- Place the symbol cards in four face-up stacks between the two players so each player can reach them.

- Players spread out the cards in a row in front of them but do not turn them over until your signal.

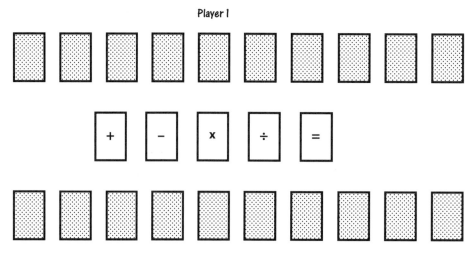

- When you say the word "Go," turn over the 3-minute egg timer. Then, the players turn over their cards.

Goal of the Game:

Be the first player to score the most points by making equations with the number cards.

Points Chart

Use all numbers = Bonus! 10 points

Use x = 5 points each

Use ÷ = 5 points each

Use + = 2 points each

Use − = 2 points each

To Begin Play:

- Each player turns the ten cards face up and moves them around to make one or more equations.

Equation Points

Continue Play:

- Players try to use as many number cards as possible to make equations until the time runs out.

- Take symbol cards as you need them to make equations.

- Pay attention to the point values.

Points Chart
Use all numbers = Bonus! 10 points
Use x = 5 points each
Use ÷ = 5 points each
Use + = 2 points each
Use − = 2 points each

Examples of equations than can be made:

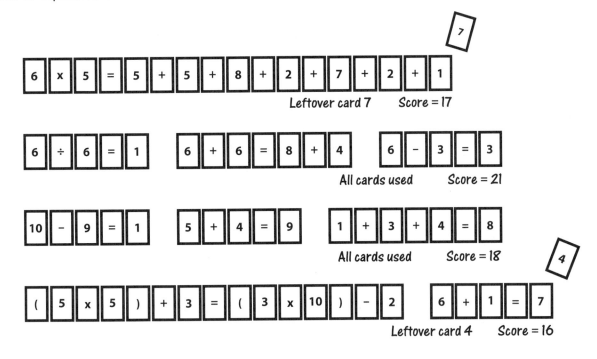

- When time is up, the dealer checks the equations and records the players' equations and score.

- Number cards not used go back into the deck. The dealer shuffles again and deals again for the next round.

Winning:

The winner is the player who has the most points when all the cards are used up or when no one can make any more equations. Play can also be ended after a given number of rounds.

0-7424-3012-X Math Card Games

Fraction Match

Concept: Understanding the meaning of fractions

Players: 2 to 4

Materials: Prepare the following ten pairs of fraction cards and associated picture cards. Some fractions are pictured as parts of a whole and others as parts of a set to give students practice with recognizing both.

Sample pairs:

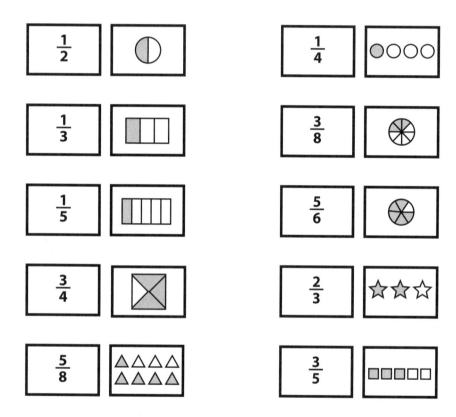

Suggestions:

- Review the meaning of fractions as a part of a whole and as part of a set.

- You may wish to prepare more pairs of fraction matches. Make enough so students can lay them out in equal rows, such as 4 rows of 8 or 6 rows of 5 for this game.

Fraction Match

Play with 2, 3, or 4 players.

Choose one person as dealer.

Dealer shuffles the cards.

How to Deal:

• Place the cards in four rows of five cards on a table so all players can see them.

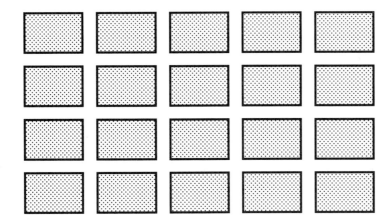

Goal of the Game:

Be the player with the most cards when all the pairs have been matched.

To Begin Play:

• The player to the left of the dealer begins.

• The player turns over any two cards and names the written or pictured fractions.

• The player looks for a match. A match is a fraction and a picture that shows the fraction.

Examples of matches:

Both say "one-third"   Both say "three-fifths"

Fraction Match

Continue Play:

• If the player uncovered two cards that show a fraction and its picture, it is a match. The player keeps the cards and puts them aside.

Example of a match:

• If you make a match, you go again. Choose two more cards.

• If your cards do not show a fraction and its picture, turn them face down again. Play passes to the left.

Hint: Pay attention and try to remember where the fractions and pictures are placed. You need a good memory for this game!

Winning:

The winner is the player with the most matched cards after all of the fraction pairs have been matched.

Fraction Fishin'

Concept: Identifying equivalent fractions

Players: 2 to 6

Materials: Prepare twelve sets or four cards. Each set of four shows equivalent in fractions. One or two of the four cards can show a picture representing the fraction.

Sample sets of four equivalent-fraction cards:

Sample set for $\frac{1}{2}$: | $\frac{1}{2}$ | $\frac{2}{4}$ | $\frac{3}{6}$ | [picture of six circles, four shaded]

Sample set for $\frac{2}{3}$: | $\frac{2}{3}$ | $\frac{4}{6}$ | [picture of bar] | $\frac{8}{12}$

Sample set for $\frac{1}{3}$: | $\frac{1}{3}$ | $\frac{2}{6}$ | [picture of circle] | $\frac{4}{12}$

Sample set for $\frac{3}{4}$: | $\frac{3}{4}$ | $\frac{6}{8}$ | $\frac{9}{12}$ | [picture of square]

Suggestions:

- *Variation 1:* For more advanced students, use four cards showing only fractions symbols and omit the pictures.

- *Variation 2:* For students less familiar with fractions, make cards with both a fraction symbol and a picture on it.

Fraction Fishin'

Play with 2, 3, 4, 5, or 6 players.

Choose one person as dealer.

Dealer shuffles the cards.

How to Deal:

• Give five cards face down to each player around the circle.

• Place the rest of the deck face down in the center of the table.

Goal of the Game:

Be the first player to run out of cards.

To Begin Play:

• Players pick up their cards and look for pairs of cards that match.

• In this game, a match is any two cards that name or show a picture of equivalent fractions.

Examples:

A number and a picture match for ½:

Two fraction cards match for ⅔:

• **Each** player puts down pairs of matching cards until he or she has only unmatched cards.

• Place the matched cards face up in front of you, so others can check for errors.

Fraction Fishin'

Continue Play:

- After all the players have put down their match-es, the player to the left of the dealer begins.

- The player asks the person to his right of a card with a specific fraction. For example, you might say "Give me one-third" or "Give me five-sixths."

Hint: You are look for a match, so ask for fractions that match one of the cards in your hand.

- If the player who is asked has such a card, he or she must give it to the player who asked for it. The player then makes the match.

- If the person asked does not have such a card, the player who asked must take a card from the top of the face-down deck. If the new card matches, it is put down.

- Play moves to the next person to the left.

Winning:

The first player to run out of cards is the winner. If two players run out of cards on the same play, it is a tie and both win.

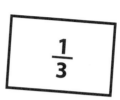

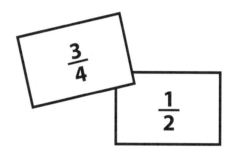

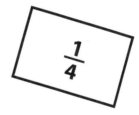

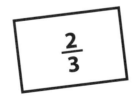

0-7424-3012-X Math Card Games

Build a Number

Concept: Understanding place value

Players: 2 or more

Materials: Three each of the following digit cards:

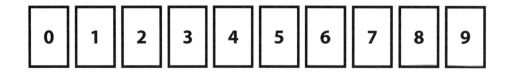

Create a grid with boxes for each digit of a three-digit number as follows:

Make multiple copies for players or have them copy the grid on paper.

Vocabulary:

Each digit in a number has a value depending on its position. This is called its *place value.*

A place-value chart:

Hundreds	Tens	Ones
3	4	5

The place-value chart shows that 345 means 3 hundreds + 4 tens + 5 ones.

Suggestions:

- Review place value with students. Give them several examples of numbers that can be formed with the same three digits, such as 345, 435, 534, 453, etc.

- Remind students that a 0 (zero) in the left most place does not change the value. 076 is the number 76.

- In this game, students try to make the greatest number, so they need to know how to compare numbers. Remind students how to compare numbers by comparing the highest place-value first.

- *Variation 1:* Use 4 sets of digit cards and a grid having four empty boxes. Students create numbers in the thousands.

- *Variation 2:* Students can use the digit cards to build the least rather than the greatest number.

Build a Number

Play with 2 or more players.

Choose one person as dealer.

Dealer shuffles the cards.

How to Deal:

• Players do not start with cards in their hands.

• Each player has a three-box grid to fill.

• Place the deck face up in the center of the table.

Goal of the Game:

Be the player to build the greatest three-digit number in your grid.

To Begin Play:

• The player to the left of the dealer goes first.

• On your turn, copy the digit on the top face-up card into any one of the three boxes in your grid.

• Then, turn the top card face-down beside the deck.

Continue Play:

• Play continues until all the players have written a digit in each of the three boxes in the grid.

• If all the digit cards are used before the boxes are filled up, the face-down deck is reshuffled, turned face up, and used again.

Hint: You have to think about where to place the digit to make the greatest number. Think ahead. Is the next number likely to be greater or less than the turned up card?

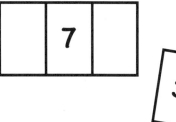

Winning:

When every player has a three-digit number written in their grids, compare the numbers. The player who made the greatest number wins.

0-7424-3012-X Math Card Games

Group 4:
Geometry and Measurement

The card games in this section provide practice with naming plane and solid figures, recognizing congruent figures, counting coins, and measuring to the nearest half-inch.

Before beginning these games, students should be introduced to the two-dimensional figures: circle, square, triangle, rectangle, pentagon, hexagon, and octagon. They should also have some experience recognizing and naming the three-dimensional figures: cube, sphere, cone, cylinder, prism, and pyramid. The most difficult may be the prism and pyramid. Tell students that the prisms may be any shape on the top and bottom, but the tops and bottoms are flat. The pyramids are flat on the bottom but come to a point on top. *Bug Off!* on page 51 shows an example of each of the figures. Page 64 has shape images that can be copied, cut out, and attached to cards.

Students should know that congruent two-dimensional figures are the same size and shape.

Likewise, students should have had experience with coins and their values, up through quarters and their values. Before using the card game, students might use play money to make certain target values in different ways. For example, using the value 27¢, students could use 1 quarter and 2 pennies, 2 dimes and 7 pennies, 5 nickels and 2 pennies, and 2 dimes, 1 nickel and 2 pennies, and so on. See coin forms on page 64, which you may copy, cut, and tape to cards.

Previous experience using rulers marked in inches and fractions of inches and rulers marked in centimeters can be reinforced by the measurement game in this section.

Bug Off! Is played like *Oops!* in the second group of games of this book. In this game, students match geometric shapes with their correct word names.

Congruent Couples challenges students to find pairs of congruent pictures in cards with a concentration-type matching game.

For *Inchworm,* students need a yardstick taped to a tabletop. Cards tell them how much to measure off along a yardstick with the goal of reaching the end of the yardstick first. A meter stick can be substituted to practice metric measurement.

Finally, *Money Target* involves using cards marked with pictures of coins to add up to some given value.

Bug Off!

Concept: Identifying geometric shapes

Players: 2 to 4

Materials: Prepare a set of paired cards. One card shows a plane or solid geometric shape. The matching card shows its name. Use the following basic shapes and names:

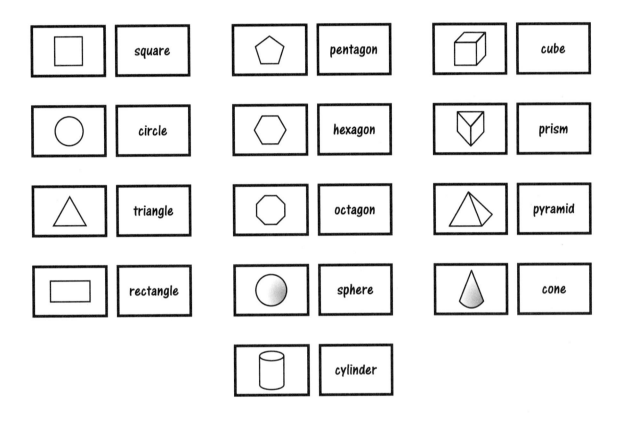

square	pentagon	cube
circle	hexagon	prism
triangle	octagon	pyramid
rectangle	sphere	cone
cylinder		

Page 64 has shape pictures that you can copy, cut out, and paste to cards. Make one additional card with a picture of a funny bug.

0-7424-3012-X Math Card Games

Bug Off!

Suggestions:

- Review the two- and three-dimensional figures that students will see on the cards.

- You may want to have students help you prepare the shape cards by drawing simple figures.

- For older students, you may want to add other cards that name additional geometric shapes or concepts, such as quadrilateral, parallelogram, trapezoid, right triangle, open figure, and closed figure, but not a polygon. Tell students to match the cards with the most specific name for the figure. For example, a card with the word *quadrilateral* should be matched only with a four-sided closed figure that has no equal sides, although squares, rectangles, parallelograms, and trapezoids are also quadrilaterals.

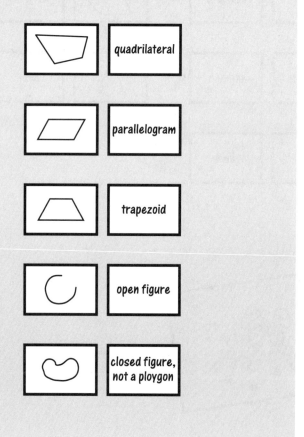

0-7424-3012-X Math Card Games

Bug Off!

Play with 2, 3, or 4 players.

Choose one person as dealer.

Dealer shuffles the cards.

How to Deal:

- Give one card to each player around the circle face down until there are no cards left.

- It does not matter if players begin with an unequal number of cards.

Goal of the Game:

Avoid being the last player who ends up holding the *Bug Off!* card.

To Begin Play:

- Players pick up their cards and look for pairs of cards that match.

A match will be the picture of a geometric shape and its name.

Here are some examples:

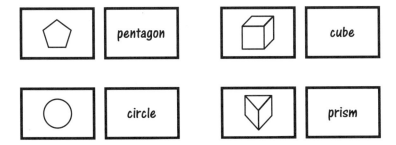

- **Each** player puts down pairs of matching cards until they have only unmatched cards

- Place the matched cards face up in front of you, so others can check for errors.

Bug Off!

Continue Play:

- After all the players have put down their matches, the dealer takes one card from the hand of the player to the right, without looking.

- If the new card can be matched with a card left in the dealer's hand, the dealer puts down that match down face up.

- Then the play moves to the player to the right.

- The player to the dealer's right takes a card from the hand of the player to the right and, if possible, pairs it with a card from their own hand.

- Play continues around the circle to the right, with each player taking a card and making a match, if possible.

- When a player loses all of their cards, they are a winner and drop out of the game.

- After a while, all of the cards will be matched except the *Bug Off!* card.

Winning:

This game has many winners and one loser—the person who ends up with the unmatched *Bug Off!* card.

0-7424-3012-X Math Card Games

Congruent Couples

Concept: Identifying geometrical and congruent shapes.

Players: 2 to 4

Materials: Prepare the ten or more pairs of cards showing congruent figures.

Sample pairs:

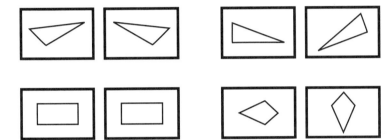

Vocabulary:

Two figures are *congruent* if they are the exact same size and shape.

Examples:

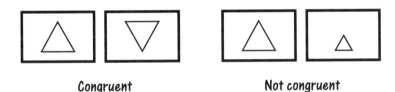

Congruent   Not congruent

Suggestions:

• Review the meaning of congruent figures with the definitions and examples above.

• It is useful to show the same figure and its match in different sizes, so students can differentiate between figures that are similar (same shape, but not the same size) and congruent (same size and same shape).

Congruent Couples

Play with 2, 3, or 4 players.

Choose one person as dealer.

Dealer shuffles the cards.

How to Deal:

• Place the cards in four rows of five cards on a table so all players can see them.

Goal of the Game:

Be the player with the most cards when all the pairs have been matched.

To Begin Play:

• The player to the left of the dealer begins.

• The player turns over any two cards. The player examines the cards to determine if they show congruent figures.

0-7424-3012-X Math Card Games

Congruent Couples

Continue Play:

- If the player uncovered two cards that show congruent figures, it is a match. The player keeps the cards and puts them aside.

Examples of a match:

- If you make a match, you go again. Choose two more cards.

- If your cards do not show congruent figures, turn them face down again. Play passes to the left.

- **Hint:** Pay attention and try to remember where the figures are placed. You need a good memory for this game!

Winning:

The winner is the player with the most matched cards after all of the congruent pairs have been matched.

0-7424-3012-X Math Card Games

Inchworm

Concepts: Measuring to quarter inches

Players: 2 or more

Materials: Find a yardstick with quarter-inch markings. Tape the yardstick to the tabletop where students will play.

Make two markers for each player. They can be small triangles cut from construction paper. It is helpful to make each pair of triangle markers a different color.

Prepare one each of the following cards:

1 in.	$1\frac{1}{4}$ in.	$1\frac{1}{2}$ in.	$1\frac{3}{4}$ in.	2 in.	$2\frac{1}{2}$ in.	$2\frac{3}{4}$ in.	$2\frac{1}{4}$ in.
$3\frac{1}{4}$ in.	$3\frac{1}{2}$ in.	$3\frac{3}{4}$ in.	$4\frac{1}{4}$ in.	$4\frac{1}{2}$ in.	$4\frac{3}{4}$ in.	5 in.	$5\frac{1}{4}$ in.
$5\frac{1}{2}$ in.	$\frac{1}{2}$ in.	$6\frac{1}{4}$ in.	$6\frac{1}{2}$ in.	$6\frac{3}{4}$ in.	7 in.	$7\frac{1}{4}$ in.	$7\frac{1}{2}$ in.
$7\frac{3}{4}$ in.	1 ft.	$8\frac{1}{4}$ in.	$8\frac{1}{2}$ in.	$8\frac{3}{4}$ in.	$9\frac{1}{4}$ in.	$9\frac{1}{2}$ in.	$9\frac{3}{4}$ in.
$10\frac{1}{4}$ in.	$10\frac{1}{2}$ in.	$10\frac{3}{4}$ in.	11 in.	$11\frac{1}{4}$ in.	$11\frac{1}{2}$ in.	$11\frac{3}{4}$ in.	

Suggestions:

- Before they begin to play, be sure students can recognize the half-inch and quarter-inch marks on the yardstick.

- Remind students that 1 foot is equal to 12 inches.

- *Variation 1:* You can adapt the number and the lengths on the cards to have students measure to the half-inch only.

- *Variation 2:* Use a meter stick in place of a yardstick. Have students identify centimeter marks on the stick. Make 24 cards representing different numbers of centimeters.

Inchworm

Play with 2 or more players.

Choose one person as dealer.

Dealer shuffles the cards.

How to Deal:

- You do not need to deal the cards.

- Place the deck face down in the center of the table.

Goal of the Game:

Be the first player to reach the end of the yardstick.

To Begin Play:

- Each player starts by putting his or her marker at the 0 point on the yardstick.

- The player to the left of the dealer begins.

- The player turns over the top card and moves their marker the length shown on the card. The place where the move ended is the new starting point.

- The card is put aside.

Example: The first player moved a marker from 0 to $1\frac{3}{4}$ inches.

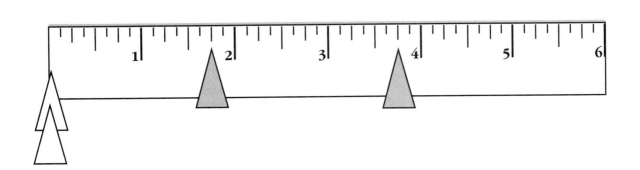

0-7424-3012-X Math Card Games

Inchworm

Continue Play:

• Play moves around the table to the left.

• The next player turns over the next card and moves their own marker the length shown on the card.

• Play continues in the same way. Each player moves their marker further along the yardstick until someone reaches the end of the yardstick. It is useful to leave a marker on the starting point and use the second triangle marker to move. Then, if you get mixed up, you can start again.

$1\frac{3}{4}$ in.   2 in.

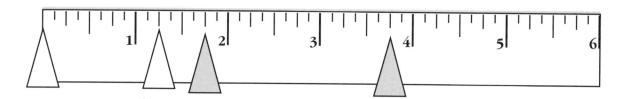

This player moved $1\frac{3}{4}$ inches on the first turn and then 2 inches on the next turn.

• If the cards are used up before a player reaches the end, the deck is reshuffled and used again.

• If other players notice a mistake that someone has made, the player who made the mistake loses that turn and must go back to their last starting point.

Winning:

The winner is the first player whose marker reaches the end of the yardstick.

Money Target

Concepts: Recognizing coins
Adding money amounts

Players: 2 or more

Materials: Prepare cards with pictures or stickers of quarters, dimes, nickels, and pennies. Page 64 has coin pictures that you can copy, cut out, and paste to cards. Make 8 quarters, 6 dimes, 10 nickels and 20 pennies. Be sure to show the front of a coin on some cards and the back of coins on others.

Suggestions:

• Before students begin, review the value of each coin. Remind them to add on to count up money. For example, if they have one quarter, 2 dimes, and 3 pennies, they would begin with 25, then add 10 twice, then add 1 three times. They would think:

25¢, 35¢, 45¢, 46¢, 47¢, 48¢

• In this game, students either choose or refuse a coin card on their turn to try to reach a target amount of money.

Money Target

Play with 2 or more players.

Choose one person as dealer.

Dealer shuffles the money cards.

How to Deal:

- Place the deck face up in the middle of the table.

Goal of the Game:

Be the player to choose money so the sum is closest to the target number by the time the deck is used up.

To Begin Play:

- The player to the left of the dealer takes the top card of the deck and places it down in their place.

- Each player must take the top card on their first turn.

Player 3

Player 2      Dealer / Player 4

Player 1

Money Target

Continue Play:

• The play continues around the circle to the left.

• Once you have your first card, on your next turn, you can choose to take or not to take the top card of the deck. If you do not use the card, you turn it face down and place it besides the deck. No one else can take the card. Then, play moves to the next player.

• You must think ahead to try to select money cards that will add up to the target amount. You must also pay attention to cards that have been refused and can no longer be played. Players try to predict what cards might still be available on their turn.

• Players can go under or over the target amount to play this game.

• Play continues until the deck is used up.

Here is an example of results after 4 players finish. The target amount is 74¢.

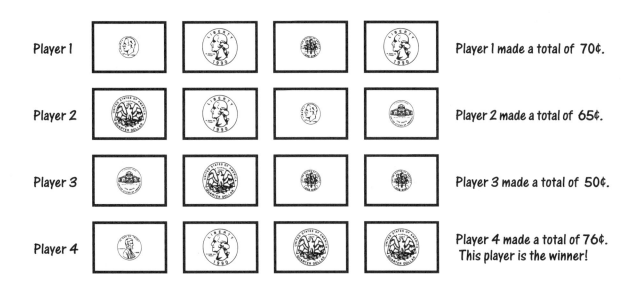

Winning:

The player whose money cards add up to a value closest to the target amount wins the game. In case of a tie, there are two winners.

0-7424-3012-X Math Card Games

Templates

Bug Off!

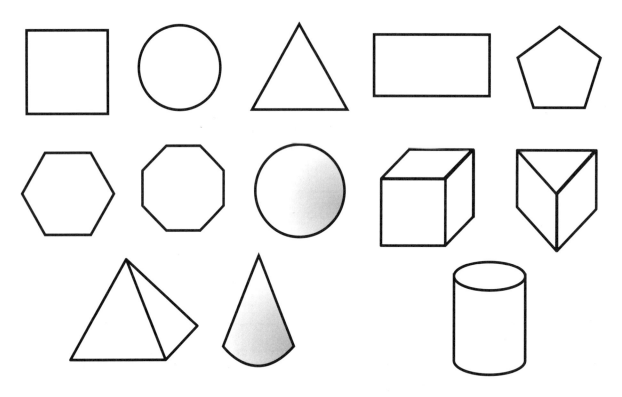

Target

Teacher Note: *You may duplicate these images and cut them out for game 14 on page 51 and game 17 on page 61.*

0-7424-3012-X Math Card Games